A CAT'S GUIDE TO THE NIGHT SKY

LAURENCE KING

This edition published in 2023
by Laurence King Publishing

First published in Great Britain in 2018 by
Laurence King Publishing

1 3 5 7 9 10 8 6 4 2

Text © Stuart Atkinson 2018
Illustrations © Brendan Kearney 2018
Design by Claire Clewley

A CIP catalog record for this book
is available from the British Library.

ISBN 978-1-510-23056-9

Printed and bound in China

Laurence King Publishing
An imprint of
Hachette Children's Group
Part of Hodder and Stoughton
Carmelite House
50 Victoria Embankment
London EC4Y 0DZ

An Hachette UK Company
www.hachette.co.uk
www.hachettechildrens.co.uk

www.laurenceking.com

Laurence King Publishing is committed to ethical and
sustainable production. We are proud participants in the
Book Chain Project ® bookchainproject.com

MIX
Paper from
responsible sources
FSC® C104740
FSC
www.fsc.org

Stuart Atkinson

A CAT'S GUIDE TO THE NIGHT SKY

illustrated by
Brendan Kearney

Laurence King Publishing

CONTENTS

BECOME A STARGAZER

Hello! My name is Felicity and I am a cat who loves to watch the stars. And you want to know more about what you can find up there in the night sky. So let me be your guide to the wonders of stargazing.

BE PREPARED

I bet you are desperate to head out and start stargazing. But if you really want to enjoy being out under the stars, there are a few things you need to know first.

WHAT YOU NEED

The best stargazing happens in winter because the Sun rises late and sets early, leaving lots of hours of darkness in between. The winter sky also has the brightest stars. But winter nights can be very, very cold. (And even summer nights can get chilly.) You will be spending a few hours outside, not moving much, so you need to make sure you can stay warm. Here are the essential things to take with you.

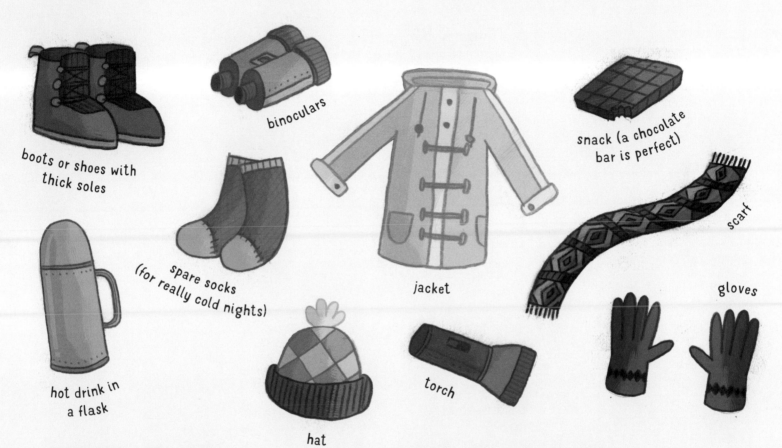

boots or shoes with thick soles

binoculars

snack (a chocolate bar is perfect)

scarf

spare socks (for really cold nights)

jacket

gloves

hot drink in a flask

hat

torch

WHERE TO GO

If you live in a place where there is a lot of light at night, it can make it hard to spot stars. So look for a dark site close to home, like:

★ A park with trees that hide the streetlights.

★ Playing fields on the edge of town.

★ A hill you can climb to get above the lights.

If you've chosen well, the sky will look darker than the view outside your door. The stars will look brighter and more colorful, they'll twinkle a lot more, and there'll be more of them.

WHO TO GO WITH

And because you'll be away from the safety of lights and other people, you need to be careful. So...

★ Always take an adult along.

★ Carry a phone.

★ Tell someone where you're going, how long you'll be, and what time you'll be back.

Now you're ready to set off on an exciting adventure of discovery!

LIGHTS IN THE SKY

NIGHT SKY IN TOWN

NIGHT SKY IN THE COUNTRY

LIGHT POLLUTION

If you live in the countryside, you can just step out your door to look at the stars. But if, like many people, you live in a town or city, you might have never seen the stars properly.

That's because of all the lights that come on at night in houses, factories, offices, shops, and streets. This light makes the sky a muddy orange color and hides the stars. Astronomers, who study the night sky all the time, call this "light pollution."

That is why you need to find somewhere really dark, where lights won't spoil the view. Once you get there you will need to wait for a while for your eyes to adjust to the night sky. After half an hour you will see more stars than you ever imagined!

WHAT WILL YOU SEE?

Once your eyes have adjusted, what will you see? Remember, the stars, planets, and even the Moon are incredibly far away. The closest things, the manmade satellites, are on average 250 miles away. So how do the Moon, planets, stars, and satellites look at such distances?

The biggest single object is the Moon. And it appears to change shape too. One night it might be a big full moon; a couple of weeks later a thin crescent.

The Moon

The planets

Our solar system's planets are millions of miles away. So they only appear as bright dots among the millions in the night sky. But there is a clever way to find the planets that I will tell you later.

There are millions of dots of light in the night sky and these are stars. To see most of them properly you need powerful binoculars or telescopes, but even with your eyes you can see several thousand.

The stars

Satellites

There are some dots of light that move quickly across the sky. These are manmade satellites—thousands of tiny spacecraft going around the Earth.

WHY LOOK AT THE SKY?

Why do people watch the sky at night? Astronomers watch the sky with big telescopes to explore our solar system, galaxy, and universe. Cats like me or people like you also watch the sky to explore what we can see beyond our planet Earth. Sometimes I watch it because it is simply amazing to watch the universe spinning round.

PEOPLE HAVE ALWAYS WATCHED THE SKY

The position of the Moon and the appearance of certain stars or groups of stars (known as constellations) often happen at the same time every year. So since ancient times, farmers have watched the night sky to know when to plant and when to harvest their crops.

In the past, unusual sights in the sky, like a strangely colored Moon, comets, or shooting stars, were believed to signal something good or bad happening. In fact, ancient astronomers were expected to interpret whether such sightings were good or bad. (And they got into a lot of trouble if they were wrong!)

Just as stars appear at certain times, they also appear in the same place in the sky. So sailors have also always used the stars to help guide them, especially when they were sailing out of sight of land.

LORDE

SHEERAN

MALALA

What's in a name?

Many of the names that the stars have date back thousands of years, mostly from ancient Greece. For the ancient Greeks, the sky was a place inhabited by gods, great heroes, and fantastic creatures. So if the shape of a constellation made them think of one of these heavenly beings, they named it after it.

The names of all the stars and constellations might seem pretty strange to us now, but for the ancient Greeks all of these names would have been as familiar as the names of A-list celebrities are to us.

WHAT ARE STARS?

All stars are hot balls of gas. And did you know that the best time to see a star is on a sunny day?

This is because our Sun is, in fact, a star! The Sun is the closest star to Earth, which is why it looks bigger and brighter than all the lights in the sky. The Sun is enormous—if the Earth was the size of a pea, the Sun would be the size of a beach ball. It is also incredibly hot (about 27,000,000°F in the middle), which is why it blazes so brightly, and can burn you even though it's 93 million miles away.

During the day the Sun is bright white, but at sunset it turns orange, and then red. It is the atmosphere between the Sun and us that makes it appear to change color.

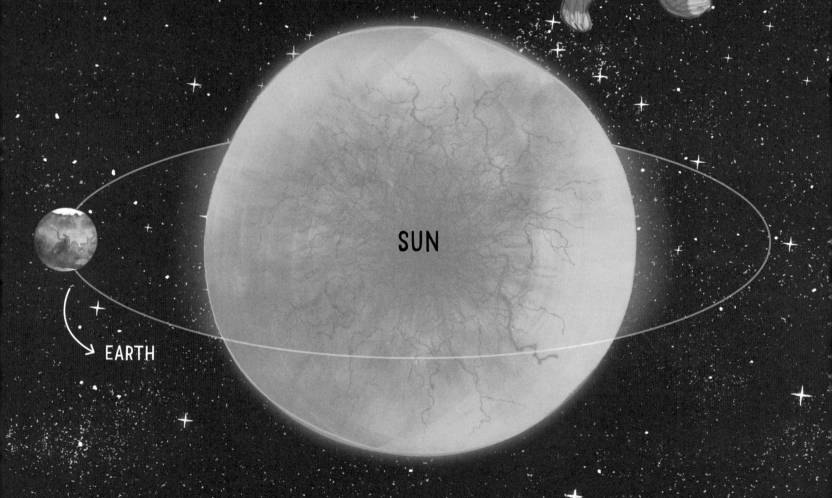

EARTH

SUN

White dwarf
83 times smaller
than the Sun

Red dwarf
20 times smaller
than the Sun

G-type
main sequence
Our Sun

Orange giant
27 times larger than the Sun

Red giant
47 times larger
than the Sun

Blue super giant
84 times larger than the Sun

Blue hypergiant
327 times larger than the Sun

Red hypergiant
2,000 to 3,000 times larger than the Sun

STAR COLORS

Although all stars are hot balls of gas, not all stars are exactly the same—some are bigger, some are smaller; some are hotter, some are cooler.

If you placed our Sun next to some of those other tiny dots in the sky, you would discover that our Sun is not the largest sun in the universe, or even our Galaxy.

In the night sky you will see red, orange, blue, and white stars. This is because these stars have different temperatures. The hottest are the white and blue ones, and the coolest are orange and red. Think of a piece of metal heating up in a fire. It starts off a dull red, then changes to orange, then white, and eventually glows blue. Stars are just the same.

Here are some of the types of stars in the sky and their relative sizes.

PATTERNS IN THE SKY

Long ago, people used the stars as a map to guide them on their journeys because the stars form patterns in the night sky. And you can use the same patterns to guide your sky-watching.

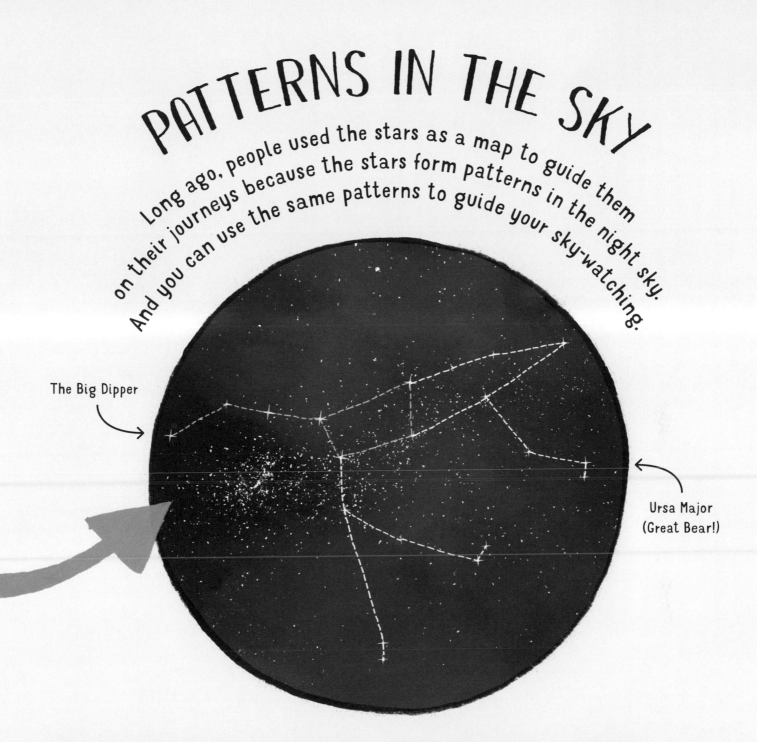

The Big Dipper

Ursa Major (Great Bear!)

LET ME INTRODUCE YOU TO TWO IMPORTANT WORDS

CONSTELLATION. This is an area of the sky with stars that, when seen together, form a pattern or shape.

ASTERISM. Within a constellation, there might be a smaller pattern of stars that catches your eye. This pattern within a pattern is called an asterism.

The Big Dipper. One asterism immediately jumps out on almost any evening of the year—the Big Dipper. Some people also call it the Plough or the Saucepan.

This set of seven blue-white stars is part of the constellation known as Ursa Major, or the Great Bear. Sky-watchers use it to "star hop"—to find their way across the constellations of the night sky.

THE DANCING SKY

When you first look at the sky, it can seem like the stars never move. But as the Earth revolves they do seem to move. It is as if they are dancing.

You might think a star has moved but it hasn't—it's the Earth that is moving! The Earth spins like a top, which means the Sun appears to rise in the east, move across the sky and set in the west, giving us day and night.

The Earth's spinning means the same thing happens with the stars. They appear in one place at the start of the evening and by dawn they will have shifted to another part of the sky.

Try picking out a star above a tree or hill and later on look at it again—it will have moved in some way: climbed higher, sunk lower, or even dropped below the horizon and vanished entirely.

The sky at the beginning of a winter's night

The sky at the end of a winter's night

The most famous star of all

There is one star that never seems to move at all. The Earth spins on an axis running between the North and South Poles, and this star always appears just above the North Pole.

So, just like the knob in the middle of a spinning top, it never seems to move at all, although everything else seems to move around it.

Because it sits above the North Pole it is called the Pole Star or the North Star. (Scientists call it Polaris.) And for the ancient sailors it was one of the most important stars because it never moved. It was their sky anchor!

It's not the brightest star in the sky, but it is pretty bright (in fact it is the 50th brightest).

the Pointers

The North Star is easy to find, thanks to the Big Dipper. The two stars in the Big Dipper's "bowl," farthest from the handle, are called the Pointers because they point towards the Pole Star.

A SKY FOR EVERY SEASON

SPRING

There's always something fascinating and beautiful to see!

Let me explain

During the day, our closest star, the Sun is so bright that we can't see any other stars in the sky. So, it is only at night, when we are facing away from the Sun, that we can see the rest of the stars.

With the other planets of our solar system the same applies—they come and go through the year depending where they and the Earth are in their orbits around the Sun.

WINTER

It was only when I'd been studying the night sky for a while that I began to realize something strange was going on. Although I could always see the Big Dipper, wheeling around the Pole Star, I could only see other stars and their patterns for a few months before they vanished.

Stars and their constellations come and go because each season has its own sky. We don't see exactly the same stars in spring as we do in summer, autumn, or winter.

SUMMER

And....

as the Earth journeys around the Sun over the course of a year, we look out at a different part of the universe in every season.

Stars that lie "above" the Earth as it rolls around, like the Pole Star and the ones that make up the Big Dipper, can be seen pretty much all year round.

AUTUMN

THE SPRING SKY

Even though the spring sky doesn't have many really bright stars, there is still plenty to see!

Of the seven main constellations in the spring sky, Leo is the one you will see first. Leo is a huge cat, so I love this constellation especially. It is named after a lion in Greek mythology that the hero Hercules fought and killed. Hydra and Cancer were also Hercules's unhappy victims. The constellation Virgo is associated with the Greek goddess of the harvest, and the smaller constellations of Corvus, Libra, and Crater were also named by the Greeks after things they thought they resembled. And these are not the only things to see in the spring sky!

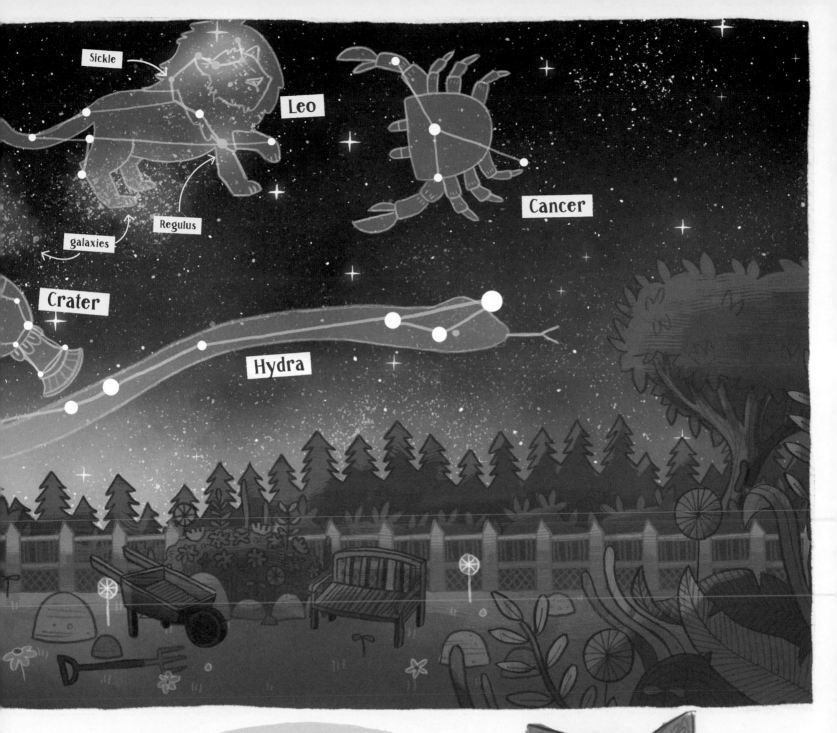

Sickle

Leo

Regulus

galaxies

Crater

Cancer

Hydra

Spring sky extras

★ There are lots of galaxies to see—especially inside Leo itself and just below Virgo. But they are very far away and you will need binoculars or a small telescope to see them properly.

★ Look out for these bright stars: Regulus in Leo and Spica in Virgo.

Turn over to meet the constellations of the spring sky.

Leo is the easiest constellation to find because it sits in the middle of the Moon's passage across the spring sky. So if you can trace that you will be able to find Leo.

Leo is actually made out of two shapes: a triangle and a back-to-front question mark. Joined together, they do actually resemble a cat lying down. The question mark is better known as the Sickle, because it looks like the tool farmers used to cut their crops.

The brightest star in Leo is Regulus, at the end of the Sickle's handle.

Leo: the Lion

In Greek mythology, the Hydra was a terrifying serpent and pet of the Greek goddess Hera that she sent to kill Hercules. But Hercules killed Hydra instead. Hydra is the largest constellation in the sky, and its long meandering line of faint stars don't catch the eye. It wriggles its way down from beneath Cancer to below Corvus and Crater.

Hydra: the Water Snake

Cancer is named after a great crab and another pet of Hera's that she sent to help Hydra. But Hercules made short work of the poor crab, kicking it right up into the sky!

The best way to find Cancer is to look for a smudge of light beyond Leo. This is M44, the Beehive Cluster, and it sits right in the middle of the constellation. Through binoculars you'll see that the Beehive is made of dozens of stars, like a swarm of bees. The rest of Cancer is an upside-down "Y" of relatively faint stars.

Cancer: the Crab

Virgo: the Maiden

Virgo is the second largest constellation in the sky. It is supposed to resemble a beautiful woman, the Goddess of the Harvest, but as we saw on the page before it looks more like a stick figure lying on its side. Virgo has one bright star, Spica, and it's an obvious blue-white color. It is actually two stars spinning around each other, but you'd need the world's most powerful telescope to see that. A normal telescope should reveal, however, lots of tiny smudges of light along the lower part of Virgo. These are incredibly far away galaxies.

Libra: the Scales

Much smaller than nearby Virgo, Libra is supposed to look like a set of old-fashioned measuring scales. I've always thought it looks more like a rocket, or a house!

Crater is a small constellation meant to represent the drinking cup (or *crater*) of the Greek god Apollo. It is hard to see because its stars are very faint. But it's always low in the sky in the northern hemisphere, visible just above trees or buildings. It is a little like a tipped-over, old-fashioned goblet, but I think it looks a lot like Corvus with a few extra stars.

Crater: the Cup

The night sky is full of bird constellations. There's an eagle, a swan, and then, below and to the right of Spica in Virgo, there's Corvus the Crow. They all make me feel hungry. Corvus is a weird-looking crow, however. It actually looks more like a squashed box...or maybe a crow with the head bitten off. Yum!

Corvus: the Crow

THE SUMMER SKY

Star hopping is easy with the big, bold constellations of the summer sky.

Summer constellations are more obvious to the naked eye than spring's. You will have to wait a bit longer to see them, however, because in the summer it isn't truly dark until midnight. And it only stays that way for a few hours. But if you don't mind losing sleep, you'll be able to enjoy the year's warmest stargazing with spectacular constellations and a lot of other celestial phenomena!

Hercules

Rasalhague

Ophiuchus

shooting stars

Scorpius

Antares

Summer sky extras

★ The best views of our galaxy, the Milky Way.

★ Lots of shooting stars in the middle of August.

★ The Summer Triangle—a trio of very bright stars, one in each constellation of Cygnus, Aquila, and Lyra.

Turn over to meet the constellations of the summer sky.

Cygnus: the Swan

For many, Cygnus is THE summer constellation, because it is overhead as darkness falls. If it's really dark you can join up its fainter stars to form a swan with outstretched wings, flying down the Milky Way. On the tip of its tail is the bright star Deneb, which marks one corner of the Summer Triangle (the other two stars in the Triangle are in Aquila and Lyra). Deneb also features in Cygnus's Northern Cross asterism (shaped like a cross!), which is formed from the five principal stars of the constellation. On a clear, dark night you'll notice a bright patch on one side of the Swan's neck. This is the Cygnus Star Cloud, made of millions of distant stars. It's an incredible sight through binoculars.

This constellation close to the Milky Way is named after the Greek god Jupiter's pet eagle. If you connect its fainter stars you can just about see its wings, but I think it looks more like a kite. Its brightest star is Altair, one of the three bright stars that make up the popular Summer Triangle asterism.

Lyra: the Lyre

Aquila: the Eagle

This tiny, compact constellation represents the lyre (harp) played by the legendary Greek poet Orpheus. Old star charts often show it held by an eagle, but all you'll see is its brightest star, beautiful blue Vega, and a little box of fainter stars beneath it. Vega shines at another corner of the Summer Triangle.

Sagittarius: the Archer

Sagittarius is seen low in the south on summer nights, but only from somewhere dark with a low horizon. It is named after an archer—not a human archer, but Chiron the centaur, a mythical half human, half horse. Like many of the creatures in the night sky, poor Chiron was attacked by Hercules.

Sagittarius's nickname is the Teapot because part of it looks like a teapot tipped down to the right, ready to pour tea. There are several interesting fuzzy patches in Sagittarius, so sweep your binoculars around and you'll eventually come across a speckly star cluster or a misty nebula (a glowing cloud of gas and dust where stars are being born).

Hercules: the Hero

If the night sky has a superhero, it is Hercules, famous for having fought many of the other creatures in the starry sky. Yet his constellation is small and a little boring. The most interesting feature is the small but beautiful Great Hercules Cluster, or M13. This looks like a tiny faint star, but a telescope reveals that it is thousands of stars packed into a ball.

Ophiucus is the ancient Greek for "Serpent Bearer," but I don't know anyone who sees a man holding a snake. It's more like a child's drawing of a house. Located off to one side of the Milky Way, the most interesting thing about Ophiucus is its brightest star, Rasalhague, on the roof peak of the house (or the eye of the serpent bearer).

Ophiuchus: the Serpent Bearer

To the right of Sagittarius lies Scorpius, named after the scorpion that killed the hunter Orion in Greek mythology. It does look like a scorpion with a stinger on its tail, but north of the equator you'll only see its head and claws because the horizon gets in the way. It's still worth looking at because its brightest star, Antares, is such a beautiful orangey red.

Scorpius: the Scorpion

THE MILKY WAY

Summer is the best time
of year to see one of the most
beautiful sights in the sky—the Milky Way.

The Milky Way is the galaxy that our Sun is part of. We are far out on a spiral arm of the galaxy, so in the summer we are in a position in our orbit around the Sun where we are looking back at the mass of our own Milky Way galaxy.

What you will see is a band of millions of stars so close together they seem to blend into one long cloud of stars. And our ancestors thought it looked like a trail of milk spilt across the sky.

The first you will perceive of the Milky Way is a long misty trail, almost cutting the sky in half. As your eyes adapt to the dark, you will see brighter areas that are big concentrations of stars. There are also dark areas, and these are dust clouds blocking the light of the stars.

In the southern hemisphere you can see the center of the Milky Way. It is so bright you can read a book by the light of it!

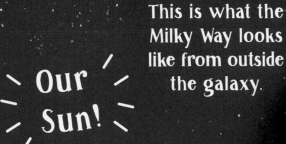

Our Sun!

This is what the Milky Way looks like from outside the galaxy.

Photographs often show the Milky Way in glorious color, with a burning yellow-orange center, and clumps and clouds of stars in blue and red. But your own eyes, even aided by binoculars or a telescope, are not sensitive enough to be able to see those colors.

When you think that these specks of light are faraway suns, many with planets of their own, you can't help but wonder...is anyone, or anything, looking back at me?

Most of the stars in the Milky Way are faint, so any light pollution, or a big, bright Moon, will drown them out. So at best you will see something that looks like a misty blue-gray cloud.

But if you look at the Milky Way against a dark sky, and use binoculars, you will see thousands of stars, like grains of salt on black paper. Don't worry about identifying anything—just enjoy all the stars.

THE AUTUMN SKY

Sky-watchers like me celebrate the start of autumn because the nights get longer and by midnight the sky is full of stars.

The main constellations of Ursa Major and Minor, Pegasus, Cassiopeia, Perseus, Andromeda, and Triangulam are large and close together with bright stars that are easy to identify. Ursa Major and Minor contain two of the most famous features of the night sky: the Big Dipper and the Pole Star. Many of the other constellations have been named after the story of the great Greek hero Perseus who rode the winged horse Pegasus and saved the beautiful Andromeda from a horrible monster.

Cassiopeia

Pegasus

Andromeda

Double
Cluster

Great Square
of Pegasus

Perseus

Triangulum

Autumn sky extras

★ The Great Square of Pegasus asterism.

★ With the naked eye, you can see a galaxy in the middle of Andromeda more than 2 million light years away!

★ Use binoculars or a small telescope to find a pair of star clusters called the Double Cluster between Perseus and Cassiopeia. They look like two piles of sugar grains.

Turn over to meet the constellations of the autumn sky.

Perseus: the Hero

Perseus was another Greek hero, so famous that a large part of the autumn sky is basically a storybook celebrating his amazing adventures. I've always thought that Perseus looks like an upside-down "Y," or a pair of scissors, but if you join up the stars in the more traditional way you (kind of) get the outline of a warrior holding a sword in one hand and the head of the hideous monster Medusa in the other. (Medusa could turn people to stone just by looking at them.) Perseus is also famous for riding Pegasus and for saving Andromeda from another horrible monster.

Many stargazers (including me) think Pegasus is the best autumn constellation. In Greek mythology Pegasus was a horse with a difference—he had wings! Pegasus was basically the way Perseus got around. With a little imagination you can join the constellation's stars up into a shape a bit like a horse flying upside down in the sky. The four brightest stars in Pegasus can be joined to make an asterism sky-watchers call the Great Square of Pegasus.

Pegasus: the Winged Horse

Andromeda: the Maiden

Poor Andromeda! She was a beautiful maiden who was chained to a rock by her parents as an offering to a hungry sea monster. Luckily Perseus and Pegasus were passing by at the time and rescued her. And as a constellation, she is just two lines extending away from Pegasus—more or less where his hind legs would be. (Maybe that is how she really escaped the sea monster—by clinging to Pegasus's legs?)

Ursa Major: the Great Bear

Ursa Minor: the Little Bear

Although the Big Dipper's constellation Ursa Major is visible all year round, autumn is the best time to see it and the Big Dipper. Simply look to the north after dark and there in front of you will be a big pan drawn with stars, its long handle on the left. (The head and legs of the bear itself are made out of quite faint stars, so you might struggle to see them unless you are somewhere really dark.)

Ursa Minor represents (surprise, surprise) a small bear! It looks like a smaller version of Ursa Major, but without the legs, which is why its brightest stars are known as the Little Dipper. The star at the end of the tail is the most important star in the whole sky—the Pole Star.

High in the east on autumn evenings you'll see a "W" of stars. This is Cassiopeia, and although it's only small it's very eye-catching. Cassiopeia can be seen throughout the year, but as the Earth rotates it seems to rotate too—so in winter it looks like more like an "M." The name Cassiopeia comes from a proud queen of Greek mythology, who was flung up into the sky for saying her daughter was more beautiful than the gods!

Cassiopeia: the Queen

Triangulum: the Triangle

Surprise, surprise, Triangulum is just three stars joined together to make a tiny triangle. But it's named after one of the tools architects used to use to measure things, not the musical instrument you are made to play at school.

THE WINTER SKY

Dress up like a polar explorer to enjoy what many stargazers say are the best skies of the year.

The cold means that the skies are much crisper and clearer than at any other time of the year. And because it gets dark earlier, you get more (and earlier) viewing time. Winter has the greatest number of bright stars, the most beautiful star clusters and nebulae, and some good meteor showers too.

Capella

Auriga

Betelgeuse

Orion

Geminid shower

Orion's Belt

Rigel

Hyades

Pleiades star cluster

Taurus

Aldebaran

Winter sky extras

★ Be ready in mid-December to watch the Geminid shower shoot meteors out of Gemini.

★ Use a telescope to examine the stars of Orion's sword (which hangs from his belt) and find the beautiful Orion nebula.

Turn over to meet the constellations of the winter sky.

Orion: the Hunter

Orion is named after a hunter from Greek mythology, and you can imagine him fighting with the mighty bull Taurus, his faithful hunting dogs (Canis Major and Canis Minor) close by.

After the Big Dipper, Orion must be the most famous star pattern in the sky, and it is very easy to spot. Just look for an hourglass of stars, with a short line of three blue stars in its middle (Orion's Belt). Orion has two of winter's brightest stars: orange Betelgeuse at top left, and icy blue Rigel to the lower right. Try and spot a shorter line of three faint stars hanging off the left side of Orion's Belt. This is his sword.

Canis Major: the Great Dog

Canis Major is often identified as one of Orion's hunting dogs. And cats don't really like hunting dogs. It is also identified with the three-headed dog in Greek mythology who guards the underworld. However, this constellation has the brightest star in the whole sky, Sirius—or the Dog Star. To find Sirius, use Orion's Belt as a guide—it points down towards the star. Sirius flashes brilliantly, like a huge diamond in the sky. This is caused by the movement of the air in our atmosphere breaking up its light.

Canis Minor: the Little Dog

This little puppy is just a pair of stars close together, so I can look at it without the fur on the back of my neck rising! The brighter of the two is called Procyon, and it's also known as the Pup.

Above and to the right of Orion you'll see an obvious "V" of stars. This is a large star cluster called the Hyades and it represents the sharp horns of Taurus attacking Orion. The blood-red star on the end of one horn is Aldebaran (the Eye of the Bull). On Taurus's shoulder is a small knot of blue stars, like a mini Big Dipper. This is another star cluster, called the Pleiades, or the Seven Sisters—if you have good eyesight you will see its seven brightest stars. If you don't, a pair of binoculars will reveal them and dozens more.

Taurus: the Bull

In Greek mythology, Auriga was the inventor of a chariot pulled by four horses. But to me it actually looks more like a big pentagon of stars, with one—yellowish Capella—brighter than the rest.

Auriga: the Charioteer

Gemini: the Twins

With a little imagination you can just see a pair of stick figures to the upper left of Orion in winter. These are Gemini—the Twins, Castor and Pollux of Greek mythology. You can often see one of the planets of our solar system passing through the same part of the sky as Gemini.

THE BEST OF THE REST

There are also a handful of other constellations to look out for, and are best seen in the summer or autumn.

Aries: the Ram

In Greek mythology, the hero Jason led a daring mission to steal a golden sheep's fleece guarded by a fearsome dragon. The zigzag line of stars that make up Aries was imagined to be the ram from whom the golden fleece was originally taken. Sometimes the orbit of a bright planet will move through the same area of the sky as Aries.

Pisces: the Fish

Thankfully, Pisces looks nothing to me like a pair of fish as it did to the ancient Greeks—otherwise it would drive this hungry cat crazy! Look beneath Andromeda's long trail of quite bright stars and you'll see Pisces's large, lopsided "V" of much fainter stars. Like Aries, Pisces will often have a "guest star" planet passing through it.

Aquarius:
the Water Carrier

This pattern of stars was associated with a boy who carried water in a jar for the ancient Greek gods up on Olympus. But I prefer instead to think of this constellation as a deflating balloon hanging from a piece of string. And like Aries and Pisces, sometimes the paths of the planets pass through the same area of the sky as Aquarius.

Bootes:
the Herdsman

Bootes lies near the Big Dipper, and stargazers enjoy finding its brightest star, Arcturus, by following the curve of the Dipper's handle. In ancient times, Bootes was imagined as a man, identified variously as a herdsman, a hunter, or the son of the Goddess of the Harvest. But to me this triangular group of stars looks like a kite with a string or an ice cream cone!

Corona Borealis: the Northern Crown

Corona Borealis is supposed to represent the crown of Ariadne, the daughter of King Minos of Crete. Although small, Corona Borealis's semicircular line of stars makes it easy to find in the night sky, and it is situated close to Hercules. And amazingly, it does look quite like a jewelled crown hanging there in the sky.

THE MOON

The Moon is probably the first thing you will ever have seen in the sky. Did you know that it is actually a big ball of rock that circles the Earth?

Moon Seas. The Moon has darker areas on its surface. These are called seas, but they don't contain water—they are vast plains of frozen lava. Depending on what part of the Earth you look at the Moon from, some people think these seas make the Moon look like it has a face. In other parts of the world, the shapes seem to suggest a rabbit.

Moon craters. The brighter spots you can see are "craters," holes formed when meteorites have hit the Moon over billions of years. You might even be able to see bright lines spreading away from some of them. These "rays" are splashes of debris left on the ground after the biggest and most recent meteorite impacts. And if you look at the Moon with binoculars or a telescope you can investigate these in even greater detail.

Moon watching. The best time to study the Moon is a few days before or after it is in its full phase. Then, using binoculars or a telescope, you can see lots of detail along the Terminator line between the sunlit and dark parts of the Moon. There are dozens of craters with their rays to be seen, as well as jagged mountain ranges and smaller seas.

The Moon's phases

Have you noticed how the Moon changes shape every month? That is because what we see of the Moon depends on what light from the Sun is reflected off the Moon's surface.

As it whirls around the Earth, and the Earth whirls around the Sun, sunlight falls on different parts of the Moon, creating what we think of as the phases of the Moon.

Because it happens with such regularity, ancient humans decided to use it as a way to measure time— and all of our earliest calendars are based off of the phases of the Moon.

Nowadays we use a solar calendar (eg. based off of our movement around the Sun), but important events like harvests are still based on the Moon's phases.

New Moon
The "new" Moon is just a dark faint circle in the sky because none of the Sun's light is reflecting off of it.

Waxing Crescent
Once light begins to be reflected off the Moon's surface, the Moon enters its second phase, and each night the sliver of light grows larger and larger.

First Quarter
The Moon's third phase occurs when the light covers fully half of the Moon,

Waxing Gibbous
In the fourth phase, the light continues to spread across the surface. Gibbous actually means an illuminated part greater than a half circle, but smaller than a full circle.

Full Moon
Once the light covers a full circle of the Moon's surface, we enter the fifth phase.

Waning Gibbous
In the sixth phase, the whole process starts to go in reverse as less and less light is reflected off the Moon's surface.

Third Quarter
In the seventh phase, the light again reaches the halfway point.

Waning Crescent
And in the eighth phase, the crescent appears again before it disappears completely to create the "new" Moon.

How the Moon was made

Did you know that the Moon hasn't always been there? Four-and-a-half billion years ago, the Earth was very different from now. Earth was still a "baby" world, a battered-looking ball of hot rock being pelted by countless other rocks from space, or meteors.

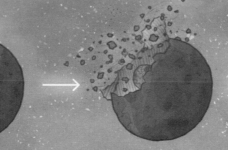

Then a particularly large meteorite, perhaps up to half our planet's size, came along.

It struck the Earth and shattered into a million million pieces. It caused quite a big smash in the Earth's surface as well.

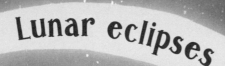

Lunar eclipses

The Earth goes around the Sun, and the Moon goes around the Earth, so sometimes they all line up with the Earth in the middle. When this happens, the Earth casts a shadow on the Moon. This is called a "lunar eclipse." If the Moon goes totally dark it's a "total lunar eclipse;" if only part of it goes dark it's a "partial lunar eclipse."

No two lunar eclipses are alike. Sometimes the Earth's shadow makes the Moon look like an orange Halloween pumpkin. Sometimes the Moon goes more the color of red wine.

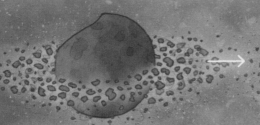

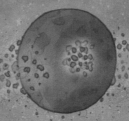

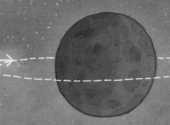

For many millions of years the shattered bits of the asteroid and the Earth floated around the Earth.

Over time all these bits came together into a kind of ring (like the rings that exist around the planet Saturn) orbiting the Earth.

And after many more millions of years, all the material in that ring began to form into a single body again. But this time one that maintained a steady orbit around the Earth.

Solar eclipses

Occasionally, the Moon passes between the Sun and Earth, blocking out the Sun. This is a "solar eclipse." In these cases, the Moon looks like a black disc against the shining brightness of the Sun.

Because looking directly at the Sun for too long can damage your eyes, you need to wear special protective lenses to watch a solar eclipse. Astronomers put special material over their telescopes to protect their eyes.

A total eclipse of the Sun is very rare, but magical. The Moon moves slowly across the face of the Sun until it vanishes, leaving just a black hole with a silvery blue halo.

Then things get weird. Birds burst into song, thinking it is dusk; the air feels chilly, and bands of shadow ripple across the ground. After a few minutes, the Sun bursts into view again, and everything returns to normal.

THE PLANETS

Much closer to us than the stars, but still very far away, are the planets of our solar system.

Mercury

Mercury is the closest world to the Sun, and this makes it hard to see. It's always very low in the eastern sky before sunrise or the western sky just after sunset. It just looks like a silvery speck of light.

Venus

Venus is the easiest planet to spot because it is by far the brightest. It is closer to the Sun than us, but much further from it than Mercury. It can be seen for several hours before sunrise (when it's known as the Morning Star) or for several hours after sunset (the Evening Star). At its brightest, Venus can cast a faint shadow behind you if you're somewhere really dark.

Mars

Although Mars is known as the Red Planet, it's not actually red. Tomatoes, cherries, and strawberries are red. Mars is more...orange! Every two years, when it's at its closest to us, Mars can be strikingly bright, especially if it's high in the sky. Then it looks brighter than any other star.

Neptune

Unfortunately, Neptune is so far away and so faint you really need a telescope to see it, and the dwarf planet Pluto needs a really big telescope!

Uranus

Uranus is so far away that it takes 84 years to orbit the Sun. It is big enough to see with the naked eye, but only if you know where and when to look, and if the sky is very, very dark. Binoculars and telescopes bring out its pale green color, but the naked eye will just see a tiny white speck.

Saturn

Saturn is also huge, but smaller and further away than Jupiter, so it's not usually as bright. On a really dark night it has a subtle yellow-gold hue.

Jupiter

Jupiter is the largest of the planets (over 1,000 Earths could fit inside it), but because it is incredibly far away, it's often not as bright as Venus or Mars. It does have its bright moments though—shining with a blue-white light.

With binoculars, you may spot some tiny "stars" close to Jupiter—two, three, and sometimes four. These are actually the four largest of Jupiter's 64 moons! The number we see changes as they whirl around the planet.

WHICH LIGHTS ARE PLANETS?

If it twinkles, it's a star. If it shines steadily, it's probably a planet!

Planets are tiny discs, but stars are just points of light, and the air moving between them and us makes this light shudder (or twinkle). If you see a bright star moving like an airplane, it's a satellite (see pages 52 and 53) or possibly an airplane really high up in the sky.

The first time I saw a planet in the sky, I didn't know it was a planet. It was brighter than any of the other stars in the sky, but it wasn't twinkling. It was just hanging there like a lantern. This star was in fact the planet Venus.

Are they stars?

No, not at all. Like the Moon, planets do not themselves produce light, they are reflecting the light of the Sun. And they are reflecting it across millions of miles of space. If you know when and where to look, you can see without a telescope many of the other planets in our solar system: Mercury, Venus, Mars, Jupiter, and Saturn. And if you have really good eyesight you might even be able to see Uranus.

WHAT ARE YOU LOOKING FOR?

You'll usually see a planet on its own, but sometimes you will see one meet up with the Moon (a "conjunction") or another planet.

Depending on where you are and the season of the year, the planets can be found in different parts of the sky. Books, magazines, and websites on stargazing should be able to provide the information on where they will be on any given night. Or there are plenty of apps you can buy for your phone or tablet.

SHOOTING STARS

One night there was a sudden streak of light in the sky.
I thought a star had fallen from the sky!

It was a shooting star, which isn't really a star at all. They are meteors—bits of space dust plunging super-fast through Earth's atmosphere. The friction makes them burn up and that creates streaks of light in the sky. They range from very faint to very bright and usually vanish in less than a second. Some are blue, green, or gold, but most are blue-white.

When the Earth's orbit takes it through a kind of river of "space dust," you'll see lots of shooting stars. Astronomers call this a "meteor shower."

There are around a dozen meteor showers every year, but some are more impressive than others. The best ones are in mid-August, late October, mid-November, and mid-December.

48

How meteor showers happen

river of space dust

Fireballs and meteorites

Sometimes larger bits of space rock enter the Earth's atmosphere. They are very bright, move more slowly, and will often flare dramatically several times before fading away. These are called "fireballs." Only a very few meteors do not burn up completely and reach the ground. They will often shine as bright as the Moon, and their arrival is usually announced by a window-rattling, bone-shaking sonic boom. Once on the ground they are known as meteorites.

THE NORTHERN LIGHTS

One October evening I had been out stargazing for a few hours when suddenly the whole of the northern sky filled with curtains of red light, fluttering and rippling wildly.

I'd just seen the famous Northern Lights! The Northern Lights (also known as the Aurora Borealis) occur when storms on the Sun's surface send gaseous material shooting out into space. If such a solar flare reaches Earth, it can react with gases in the atmosphere and Earth's magnetic field, causing the gases to glow as different colors and form shapes.

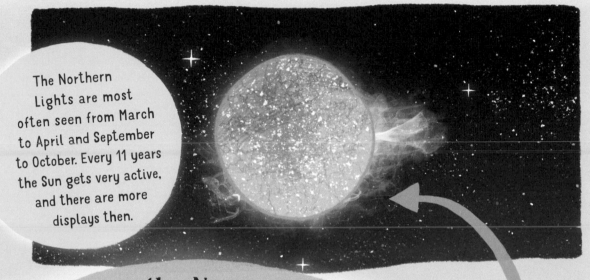

The Northern Lights are most often seen from March to April and September to October. Every 11 years the Sun gets very active, and there are more displays then.

Catching the Northern Lights

If you live near the North or South Pole you will see the Northern Lights regularly—because they are concentrated there. Occasionally they are visible away from the poles, as far south as France or the northern United States in the northern hemisphere. And as far north as Australia in the southern hemisphere. It really depends how much of a battering the Earth is getting from the Sun's flares.

If you get a chance to see the Northern Lights near you, then the first you will probably see is a green rainbow, with gray-white rays or beams pointing up from it, fading in and out. If you're really lucky you'll see some bright curtains of red light that look like they're dancing in the sky, rippling, and swaying to and fro.

Big solar storms can happen at any time. There are satellites that watch the Sun 24 hours a day, and spot solar storms as they happen. So they give us a few days' warning. Lots of websites share these warnings, and you can also get an app for your phone or tablet that will alert you.

MOVING LIGHTS IN THE SKY

You might notice on a clear night dozens of lights crossing the sky in all directions. They look like stars that have cut themselves free and are soaring away.

They're not stars, and they're not alien spaceships spying on us (probably)! They are manmade satellites—small spacecraft orbiting the Earth many hundreds of miles away, glinting as they catch the Sun's light.

There are many satellites up there. And they are used for all sorts of things:

★ Car GPS systems use them to plan routes.

★ Weather forecasters use the pictures they take to predict our weather.

★ Cell phones use them to relay calls and text messages.

The International Space Station

The brightest satellite you'll see is the International Space Station, or ISS. Astronauts from lots of different countries live for months onboard it, practicing together how they'll fly to Mars in the future or doing experiments in zero gravity or photographing the Earth as it rolls beneath them.

The ISS isn't visible every night. It comes and goes. There are websites and apps that will give you dates and times for sightings near you. They'll also tell you when you can see other, smaller spacecraft—some carrying cargo, others carrying people—flying up to or back from the ISS.

Satellites

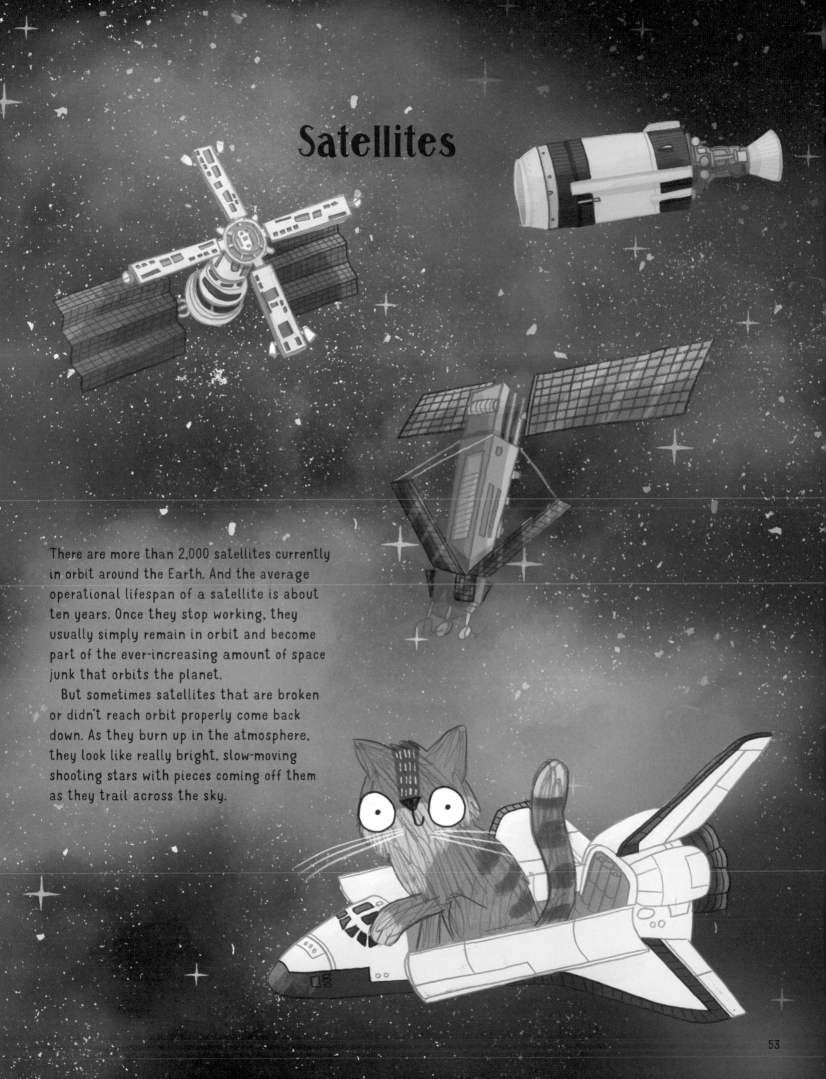

There are more than 2,000 satellites currently in orbit around the Earth. And the average operational lifespan of a satellite is about ten years. Once they stop working, they usually simply remain in orbit and become part of the ever-increasing amount of space junk that orbits the planet.

But sometimes satellites that are broken or didn't reach orbit properly come back down. As they burn up in the atmosphere, they look like really bright, slow-moving shooting stars with pieces coming off them as they trail across the sky.

FUZZY PATCHES

When you are out watching the night sky, you might notice some bits of the sky that look, well...a bit fuzzy. That is because these objects are incredibly far away, and astronomers call them "deep sky objects." But a lot of stargazers like you just call them "faint fuzzies."

As the name implies, you don't see a lot of detail in faint fuzzies, but photos of them can reveal their true beauty. They are usually taken through big telescopes, then processed with computers to bring out the detail. Faint fuzzies are much farther away than the stars you can see and they are also much, much larger. You'll need binoculars or a telescope to see most of them.

FAINT FUZZIES
are often one of three things:

1. Galaxies

Some faint fuzzies are actually other, neighboring galaxies. The world's most powerful telescopes have revealed an estimated 100 billion galaxies besides our own. And that number is likely to go up as telescopes get ever more powerful!

2. Nebulae

And some faint fuzzies are nebulae—enormous clouds of gas and dust, far, far out in space. Some glow because there are stars hidden inside them. Some shine because they reflect the light of nearby stars. And some shine because stars are being born inside them.

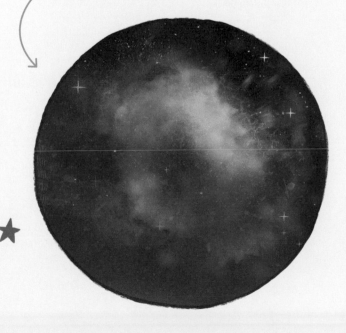

3. Clusters

Some faint fuzzies are star clusters. Most stars are part of a pair, a trio, or a larger group, or "cluster" of stars. "Open clusters" contain dozens or even hundreds of stars, which all formed at the same time, in the same place. Globular clusters are huge balls of very, very old stars, millions all packed together like a bee swarm. But they are so distant that you need binoculars or a telescope to see them.

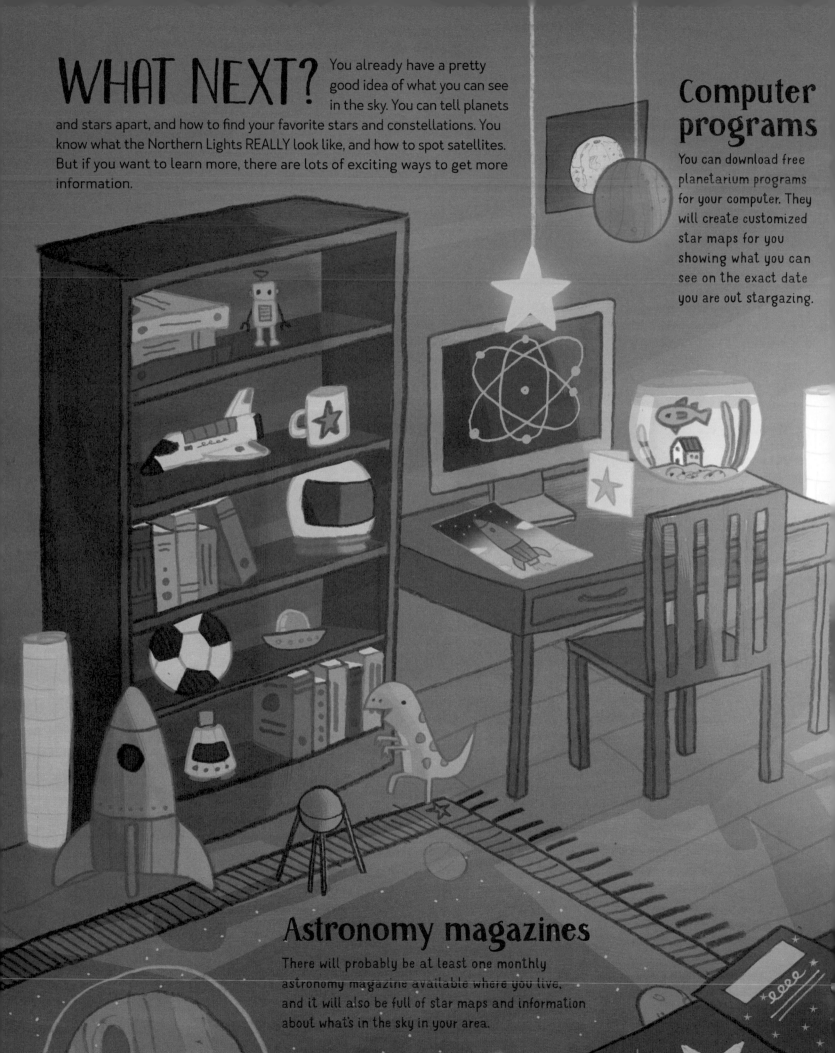

WHAT NEXT?

You already have a pretty good idea of what you can see in the sky. You can tell planets and stars apart, and how to find your favorite stars and constellations. You know what the Northern Lights REALLY look like, and how to spot satellites. But if you want to learn more, there are lots of exciting ways to get more information.

Computer programs

You can download free planetarium programs for your computer. They will create customized star maps for you showing what you can see on the exact date you are out stargazing.

Astronomy magazines

There will probably be at least one monthly astronomy magazine available where you live, and it will also be full of star maps and information about what's in the sky in your area.

Star atlas

A star atlas contains detailed maps of the night sky, with all the stars and constellations labeled, and the positions of hundreds of star clusters, nebulae, and galaxies.

Astronomy apps

If you have a cell phone or tablet there are hundreds of astronomy apps available. Some tell you when the ISS will cross the sky, when a meteor shower will be at its best, or when you'll see an eclipse. The best ones are the "planetarium apps," which show you what's in the sky for a chosen date and time.

So get excited! Armed with all this knowledge, you will be able to look up and see the stars not as dots in the sky, but as friends—friends you will have for the rest of your life.

LET'S GO!

Now you are a fully qualified stargazer.

When setting out on your stargazing adventures, always remember to plan ahead. Know where you want to go, who you are going with, and what you are going to look for. Every night sky offers its own adventure, from satellites to shooting stars, from the Big Dipper to the Milky Way. Let the constellations be your guide.

GLOSSARY

★ ASTERISM
An obvious group of stars within a constellation.

★ ASTRONOMER
A scientist who studies the night sky.

★ AURORA
The interaction of flares from the Sun with gases in our atmosphere. The Northern Lights (the Aurora Borealis) is the most famous aurora.

★ CONJUNCTION
When two bodies appear to meet in the night sky.

★ CONSTELLATION
An area of the sky supposed to represent a character, creature, or object from ancient myths or stories.

★ CRATER
Pits made on the surface of the Moon by meteorites.

★ DARK ADAPTATION
The time it takes for your eyes to adjust to the darkness of a night sky.

★ FAINT FUZZY
Distant objects visible as patches of fuzzy lights.

★ FIREBALL
A very bright shooting star that moves slowly across the sky and that flares dramatically before fading away.

★ GALAXY
A vast, gravitationally bound, system of stars (billions of them). Our galaxy is the Milky Way.

★ INTERNATIONAL SPACE STATION
Or ISS. Currently the largest manmade satellite and a center for astronauts of many different countries.

★ LIGHT POLLUTION
The lights from our manmade environment that make viewing the night sky difficult.

★ LUNAR ECLIPSE
The moment when the Sun, Earth, and Moon are aligned in such a way that the Earth casts a shadow on the Moon.

★ METEOR/SHOOTING STAR
A meteor is a bit of matter from space that, when it enters the Earth's atmosphere, usually burns up, and thus creates a shooting star. There are two kinds of shooting star: fireballs and meteors.

★ METEOR SHOWER
When the Earth's orbit takes it through a trail (or "river") of space rock left behind by a comet that then burns up as meteors in the atmosphere.

★ METEORITE
A piece of a meteor that doesn't actually burn up in the atmosphere, but that lands on the planet's surface as a rock or piece of metal (or a mixture of the two).

★ NEBULA
An enormous cloud of gas and dust far out in space.

★ NORTHERN LIGHTS

The Aurora Borealis. See Aurora.

★ OPEN CLUSTER

A grouping of dozens or even hundreds of stars.

★ ORBIT

The path of a planet or star. The Earth orbits around the Sun, and the Sun follows an orbit in the galaxy.

★ PHASES OF THE MOON

The different shapes that the Moon appears to take (from crescent to full) over the course of a month, as the Sun's light reflects on it from different angles.

★ PLANET

A mass of material, rounded by its own gravity, that orbits a star. The Earth is one of eight planets orbiting our Sun.

★ POLAR AXIS

The term referring to the line on which the Earth spins.

★ SATELLITE

Any object that orbits a planet. The Moon is the Earth's largest satellite, but there are also many, much smaller, manmade satellites that orbit our planet, such as the International Space Station (ISS).

★ SOLAR ECLIPSE

When the Moon passes between the Sun and the Earth.

★ SPACE JUNK

Term used for all the many no-longer-functioning manmade stuff that continues to orbit our planet.

★ SPACE ROCK

The stuff that meteors are made of.

★ STAR ATLAS

A book of maps of the night sky seen at different times of the year and at different places on the planet.

★ STAR CLUSTER

A subgroup of stars within a galaxy that are gravitationally bound to each other.

★ STAR HOPPING

When you move from looking at one group of stars to another in the night sky.

★ SUN/STAR

Gigantic hot balls of gas.

★ TERMINATOR

The line between the sunlit and dark parts of any object in our solar system.

INDEX

Dedications

This book is dedicated to three individuals. Firstly, to the memory of Félicette, a stray cat plucked from the streets of Paris in 1963 to become the first cat to go into space. For some reason, Félicette's story is nowhere near as well known as the story of Laika, the first dog to go into space. Recently there has been a campaign to build a statue to Félicette's memory, and I hope readers of this book will take some time to learn about her. Of course, Felicity is named after Félicette...

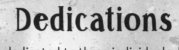

Secondly, it is dedicated to Peggy, a beautiful rescue cat we said a sad goodbye to last year. Peggy had a terrible start in life, but after coming to us she was happy and her life was full of love. Peggy inspired this book when, one night camping up at Kielder Star Camp, I took her outside and she looked up at the starry sky with real curiosity on her face, and I wondered how many cats spend their nights looking up at the night sky and appreciate its beauty...

And finally, it's dedicated to Stella, who shines more brightly in my eyes than all the stars in the sky combined.

Many thanks to Donald, Chloë, Brendan, Claire, and everyone at Laurence King for working so hard to make this book possible—and to the always-amazing "L," who made it happen in the first place.

Stuart Atkinson